WINDMILL HILL WADDESDON

ARCHITECTURE, ARCHIVES & ART

COLIN AMERY

WITH PIPPA SHIRLEY & STEPHEN MARSHALL

Colin Amery is an architectural critic and historian and Founding Director of the World Monuments Fund in Britain.

Pippa Shirley is Head of Collections at Waddesdon Manor.

Published in 2011 by
The Rothschild Foundation
Waddesdon Manor
Waddesdon
Near Aylesbury
Buckinghamshire
HP18 0JH
www.waddesdon.org.uk

ISBN 978-0-9547310-6-9

Designed by Libanus Press, Marlborough
Printed by Hampton Printing (Bristol) Ltd

Lord Rothschild
by Lucian Freud

FOREWORD

I have always seen Waddesdon as a centre for excellence in all aspects of our cultural heritage. Our visitors clearly share my enthusiasm for the beauty of the house and appreciate the immense care that goes into the maintenance of the whole estate. The vision of my cousin Mrs James de Rothschild was always to ensure that Waddesdon, a magnificent example of a Rothschild house and collection, would be preserved in perpetuity for the enjoyment of the public. I have always sought to honour her vision funding both restoration and improvements, and insisting on the highest possible standards.

This catalogue and accompanying exhibition mark the opening of a new building on Windmill Hill, at the heart of the Waddesdon Estate, which will be the new home for the archives of the Manor, the estate and the family papers of the Rothschilds who have, for four generations, been responsible for Waddesdon. My intention is for Windmill Hill to become a centre of study, research and outreach in the fields of the arts, collecting, heritage and conservation and also the environmental and horticultural concerns that affect our world. The new buildings replace a redundant dairy farm and their new use reflects the continuing dynamism of a changing estate.

The Rothschild Foundation will be based there to continue our philanthropic interests which give grants to a wide range of charitable activities across many sectors.

These will include education and social welfare, arts heritage and culture, as well as 'green' environmental and sustainable development research. The programme to help local good causes in the Vale of Aylesbury will continue.

The remarkable new building at Windmill Hill has been carefully designed to enhance the landscape and it is my hope that as many people as possible will enjoy it as the setting for debate and conferences across a variety of cultures and disciplines. This exhibition and catalogue also show my own particular concern to raise standards in contemporary architecture and the conservation of our heritage. Since the centenary restorations of the house in 1994 I have, I hope, demonstrated at Waddesdon that it is rewarding and possible to combine careful conservation with the commissioning of contemporary art, furnishing and sculpture. There has always been a creative energy present at Waddesdon and Windmill Hill in its beautiful setting is the latest significant witness to this spirit.

Jacob Rothschild

Rothschild

May 2011

A TRADITION OF GOOD PATRONAGE

INTRODUCTION

Enlightened patronage is the key to good architecture and this is apparent wherever you look at Waddesdon. The recent opening of the new home for The Rothschild Foundation on a rural site at Windmill Hill on the Waddesdon estate is an outstanding example of contemporary patronage. The present Lord Rothschild has always taken a serious personal interest in both new architecture and the conservation and enhancement of his considerable inheritance. Internationally, the Rothschild family have always been builders and the English branch of the family concentrated their building activity in and around the Vale of Aylesbury – a tradition that continues to this day. By the late 1880s there were seven significant Rothschild houses in Buckinghamshire – Mentmore Towers, Waddesdon, Tring Park, Ascott, Halton, Eythrope and Aston Clinton.

Ascott   Halton

Tring Park   Mentmore Towers   Aston Clinton

Details of Rothschild houses in the Vale of Aylesbury from a painting by Jean-Marc Winkler commemorating the 1994 restoration

Today, while Waddesdon is recognised as the only major surviving example of *le style Rothschild* with its intact art collections and furniture, it is also a something of a fruitful nurturing ground for the present Lord Rothschild's collecting and building enthusiasms. He has a finely honed interest in architecture which he has exercised in his public life both in the United Kingdom and Israel and more widely internationally as a member and Chairman of the jury of the prestigious Pritzker Prize for Architecture.

The Pritzker Prize for Architecture has, since its foundation in the late 1970s, been regarded as the Nobel Prize for very high levels of architectural achievement. In some cases it is awarded for a lifetime's work and in others for outstanding design originality observed as an architectural talent matures. With early advice from such luminaries as the late Lord Clark of *Civilisation* fame, the Pritzker family, through their Hyatt Foundation, have sought the advice of distinguished authorities in architecture to be members of their international jury. Lord Rothschild was selected in 1987 and was Chairman from 2003 to 2004.

As the jury takes enormous trouble in reviewing the architectural scene it becomes an intense educational process for members of the jury. During his time on the jury Lord Rothschild shared in the selection of architects as diverse as the Japanese Kenzo Tange, the American Robert Venturi, the Spaniard Rafael Moneo and England's Lord Foster. In his year as Chairman the opportunity was taken to reward the lifetime's work of the architect of the Sydney Opera House – Jorn Utzon – in 2003. Lord Rothschild in the citation described the Danish architect as the man, 'who created one of the great iconic buildings of the twentieth century and throughout his life worked fastidiously, brilliantly, quietly and with never a false or jarring note.' In 2004 the flowering achievement of architect Zaha Hadid was acknowledged and she was well described by Lord Rothschild as 'someone who has shifted the geometry of buildings and is always inventive.' The Pritzker is one of the best architectural educations you can have – looking at cycles of achievement trains the eye and informs critical faculties. It may also encourage an appetite for patronage.

Looking over his shoulder at the 42 houses built by all branches of the Rothschild family during the nineteenth century in Germany, France, Austria, Switzerland, Italy, the Czech Republic and the United Kingdom, Lord Rothschild must feel a sense of building history. As so many of them have disappeared or been destroyed, the impetus to maintain Waddesdon and to add to its architectural inheritance is very strong. This publication, while it concentrates principally on a recent commission at Windmill Hill on the Waddesdon estate, also shows architectural achievements elsewhere that have informed the commissioning spirit.

Gold medal awarded to Pritzker Prize Laureates

11

Front to St. James's Park of the Rt. Honble. Earl Spencer's.

Elevation vers St. James's Park. Mais. Monseigneur le Comte de Spencer.

Spencer House, the garden façade (from *Vitruvius Britannicus* – 1767) by John Vardy 1756

SPENCER HOUSE, LONDON

Away from Waddesdon, one of Lord Rothschild's most remarkable achievements was
to make a commercially viable success of the rescue and restoration of Spencer House, the
last great neo-classical family mansion left in central London. Spencer House's rescue is a
very personal achievement. The house was familiar to him, being opposite the headquarters
of the J. Rothschild group of companies' offices in St James's Place. He had witnessed its
sad decline and conversion into offices, but he also saw the possibilities for an imaginative
restoration that his companies would find commercially sustainable. It is rare to find the
qualities of an aesthete combined with business acumen – although not so rare in much
of the Rothschild family – and vividly demonstrated by the present Lord Rothschild.

Spencer House stands overlooking Green Park in the heart of St James's and today
continues to inspire through both its visual appearance and its particular history. Built in the
1750s for the first Earl Spencer by the architect John Vardy (1718–1765), a disciple of William
Kent (*d.*1748), it was later completed by James 'Athenian' Stuart (1713–1788) – who worked
on the interiors of the first-floor rooms between 1759 and 1765.

The house demonstrates in a remarkable way the change from the Anglo–Palladian style
of Vardy and the application of the latest *gusto Greco* encouraged by the Society of Dilettanti
in much of the interior decoration. James Stuart had returned from the Grand Tour and
published in 1762, *The Antiquities of Athens measured and delineated by James Stuart and*

Nicholas Revett, painters and architects. Spencer House became a kind of built propaganda that encouraged the spread of neo-classicism.

The Spencer family had occupied the house until 1926 and subsequently there were a variety of occupants including the Ladies Army and Navy Cub until 1943, Christie's the auctioneers and, until RIT Capital Partners acquired the lease in 1985, the *Economist Intelligence Unit.* Just before and during the Second World War, the Spencers removed from the house important marble fireplaces, major doors and fittings to their estate at Althorp in Northamptonshire – saving them from the blitz.

The rescue of the sad, divided and wrecked house has been acknowledged as the finest restoration and conservation project in the UK. Incredible care and concern has been lavished on the house and 2011 marks twenty years since the completion in 1991. It was decided to restore the house back to the condition it would have been in when the architect Henry Holland (1745–1806) made some internal alterations for the second Earl Spencer between 1785 and 1792. In addition to the extensive and carefully researched historical restoration, the house has been enhanced by purchases of furniture and pictures associated with the house, and important loans secured from the V&A, the Royal Collection, the Tate and the Royal Academy.

The challenge of Spencer House was to make it work as a restored eighteenth-century town palace, almost the last one left in London, while refurbishing and equipping a substantial part of it as efficient offices for the twenty-first century. It must have been quite a task to persuade business partners that the house could be restored and used as a company head office and the state rooms also used to generate income. There was also the task of securing the support of the entire heritage bureaucracy – but Lord Rothschild's conviction, and the help of a mass of informed expert advisers, won the day and a

The Great Room by James 'Athenian' Stuart

The Palm Room by Vardy

120-year lease from the Spencer Trustees was granted.

The remarkable state rooms were restored after immense research and measuring and recording visits to Althorp to plan the making of replica marble fireplaces, wooden chair rails, door furniture and careful repair of two of the most extraordinary rooms in Britain – Stuart's unique Painted Room and the Palm Room with its gilded tree-framed niches.

It is right to think of Spencer House as a temple of the arts and, while the approach of Lord Rothschild has been to insist on the most authentic restoration that is possible, he was anxious also to provide a setting for art works of real quality and authenticity. Cipriani and Reynolds's full length portraits, for example, were chosen for the Great Room and Gavin Hamilton's *Agrippina* has been lent by the Tate to hang in the dining room, where it probably originally hung. Grand Tour sculpture belongs in the house and a recent purchase of Guercino's *King David* from a Spencer sale has restored the painting to its original home. It is seeing the house as a whole, and having the ability to acquire and furnish and maintain a momentum of collecting, that continues to give Spencer House renewed life.

King David by Il Guercino (1651), recently acquired and restored to its original home

THE NATIONAL GALLERY, LONDON

From 1985 to 1991 Lord Rothschild was Chairman of the National Gallery – perfect timing for someone as interested in the building and its expansion as he was in the national collection. In 1985 the three Sainsbury brothers, Lord Sainsbury of Preston Candover, Sir Timothy Sainsbury and the Hon. Simon Sainsbury had pledged to fund a new building on the site adjoining the Gallery, which would fill the whole site and remove any necessity to site new gallery space on top of commercial offices. The new building, to be called the Sainsbury Wing, was to display the entire early Renaissance collection.

It was a controversial moment in the history of the National Gallery and one which inspired the new Chairman to find a solution that would satisfy donors, the curators and the architectural community. An earlier architectural competition had been organised by the Board in 1982 to fit a building onto the Hampton site that would be part National Gallery and part commercial. The winning design by architects, Ahrends, Burton and Koralek was heavily criticised and led to the attack from HRH the Prince of Wales, at a dinner in May 1984 to mark the 150th anniversary of the Royal Institute of British Architects, referring to the design as, 'a monstrous carbuncle on the face of a much loved and elegant friend.' The second competition to build a completely funded building devoted to the Gallery was by invitation once an international short list had been carefully prepared.

A fact-finding tour of new art galleries in Europe and America was held for the gallery

Opposite: The Sainsbury Wing, opened after a major architectural competition in 1991

Rooms designed by E M Barry restored in the 1980s to their original colour schemes

The Rothschild Hall restoration funded by Lord Rothschild

and advisers and donors. The shortlisted architects then presented their schemes and the donors had the final choice with guidance from the assessors and the Chairman. The American team of Robert Venturi and his wife Denise Scott-Brown were chosen. They designed the eclectic but respectful neighbour to the Gallery designed by William Wilkins (1778–1839), with a sequence of fine galleries, clearly inspired by Sir John Soane's gallery at Dulwich. Other sources relate to the Brunelleschi-inspired use of *pietra serena,* and the stair that elevates the journey to the gallery floor has a sense of a *scala reggia.*

As Chairman and as a philanthropist Lord Rothschild took a great interest in upgrading the galleries and finding significant donors, who for the first time were given naming opportunities. The new era of private philanthropy flourished under his chairmanship. He personally oversaw the restoration of the fine rooms designed by E M Barry (1830–1880), removing the Ministry of Works lighting and 1960s decoration. The Chairman understood the change of taste that made it possible to restore the authentic colour schemes and reveal the classical detailing of the older galleries. The restoration of the Rothschild Hall at the top of the entrance stairs is named to acknowledge both his donation and a transforming period of chairmanship. It made possible a subsequent restoration in 2005 of the main halls that continued the trend of revealing the original colour schemes by John Dibblee Crace (1838–1919) – once so out of fashion.

Robert Venturi's vista into the Renaissance galleries of the Sainsbury Wing

North elevation of the Supreme Court with the Knesset building behind

THE SUPREME COURT, JERUSALEM

There is a deep, moving and profound Rothschild connexion with Israel that has continued for well over a century through the beneficent activities of family foundations, especially Yad Hanadiv. The decision to follow the gift of the Knesset (Parliament) building with the completely funded provision of a magnificent Supreme Court in Jerusalem, which opened in 1992, marked the hundredth anniversary of the work of Baron Edmond de Rothschild (1845–1934), in Eretz Yisrael and the establishment of the first agricultural colonies.

The decision to build on a site close to the Israeli Parliament cemented the twin ideals of justice and democracy in a visible way that made it essential that the new Court building should be of the highest architectural standard. Lord Rothschild, as Chairman of the Trustees of Yad Hanadiv, established the parameters of a two-stage international architectural competition to select a design. The first stage was open to all Israeli architects, followed by a second stage (held in the summer of 1986) that included six firms selected by invitation – three Israeli and three international firms. The winners of the competition were a brother and sister Israeli architectural team, Ada Karmi-Melamede and Ram Karmi.

Intense discussions took place between all the final entrants and the international jury. The building had both a practical and symbolic brief and it had to respond to the special urban characteristics of Jerusalem. A quotation from the winning team explained how the architects saw the special nature of Jerusalem:

'Throughout the world monumentality is congruous with power. But not in Jerusalem. Here there is a sense of the "unknown" rather than of power. You look at buildings, parts of which are hidden from view by the city wall. You see their skyline but not where they touch ground. You always retain the sensation of hidden layers and indefinite heights. This imparts a certain mystique to the buildings. Anywhere else it would be called monumentality.'

The completed building is undoubtedly redolent, in its forms and pattern of walls, of the elements that define the Old City. It sits in an amphitheatre of land with the courtrooms anchored into the sloping land. The entry 'gate' is an abstraction of the Old City's Jaffa and Damascus gates and it is the first indication that this is a building that has evolved an

Paul Benney's 1992 sketch for a painting to mark the building of the Supreme Court, showing the architects discussing the model with Government ministers including Prime Minister Yitzhak Rabin and Shimon Perez, the board of Yad Hanadiv and Lord Rothschild.

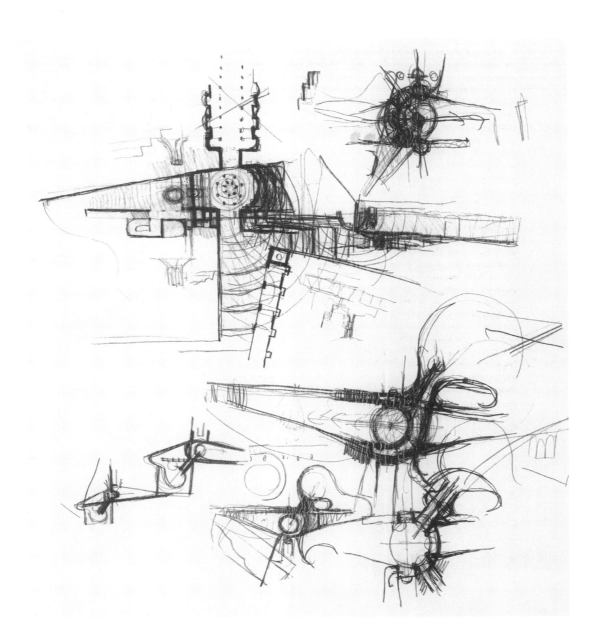

Preliminary design proposals by Ada Karmi – Melamede and Rarn Karmi

The Court is constructed of dressed white Israeli limestone

The main gateway of the Court overlooks the old gateways of the city of Jerusalem

architectural language that is rooted in the history of the city's stone buildings. From the judges' level the panoramic views of the city give a sense of what the architect, Ram Karmi calls, 'Jerusalem in the palm of one's hand' – an appropriate overview for the administrators of the law. The city looking up at the Court sees strong but varied elevations united in the use of dressed white Israeli limestone from Mitzpe Ramon. The stone has been chiselled to bring out the variety of hues and textures, rougher at the base and refined as the building rises. The building is one of the finest judicial complexes in the world, judged by the highest international standards. It stands as a powerful cultural and visual symbol. It embraces the rituals of impartial justice while absorbing the architecture and timeless traditions of Jerusalem itself.

Court Room number three – the largest in the Supreme Court

WADDESDON ESTATE

The building of Waddesdon Manor to designs by the French architect Gabriel-Hippolyte Destailleur (1822–1893) lasted from 1877 to 1883. The client, Baron Ferdinand de Rothschild (1839–1898), had acquired an estate with no house, garden or park. He had a romantic view of the Valois chateaux of the Loire Valley and what we see today is largely his vision. It was a brave and very European view of what a country house should be and the baron and his architect pulled it off. Waddesdon is not like anywhere else – it is unique and its qualities are cherished by the present Lord Rothschild. He inherited from his childless cousin, Dorothy de Rothschild in 1988, a house which, with 165 acres, was owned by the National Trust but handsomely endowed by the family and continually funded from family trusts. Like his cousin, the present Lord Rothschild is devoted to the management and enhancement of the house, collection and estate, and to making every aspect accessible to a wider public.

His intellectual and aesthetic energy applied to Waddesdon has meant that the Manor has not just been maintained and restored – it is continually being reinvigorated. The latest scheme, which this exhibition and book is designed to mark, is the new building at the heart of the estate – on Windmill Hill – where charitable and philanthropic activities will be based alongside the archives of the Manor, estate and family that chart the history of all concerned with the creation of Waddesdon, and the archives of Yad Hanadiv outside Israel. This centre

The Manor with its restored 19th-century Parterre, seen from the south

Baron Ferdinand de Rothschild with his poodle, Poupon

Mrs James de Rothschild in the Morning Room at the Manor

of excellence, fully accessible to scholars, is like a concentration of the values that created the house and collections.

There are similarities to be noted between Baron Ferdinand and the present Lord Rothschild – they are both driven by a sense of fastidious perfectionism and they are both fuelled by a strong sense of aesthetics. Baron Ferdinand was not optimistic about the long-term future of Waddesdon, and in the year before he died he wrote:

> 'Time must be relied upon to improve the house by colouring the masonry and giving it that rich mellowness of tone which age alone can produce, and beautify the grounds by allowing the trees to grow and expand. A future generation may reap the chief benefit of a work which to me has been a labour of love, though I fear Waddesdon will share the fate of most properties whose owners have no descendants, and fall into decay. May the day yet be distant when weeds will spread over the garden, the terraces crumble into dust, the pictures and cabinets cross the Channel or the Atlantic, and the melancholy cry of the nightjar sound from the deserted towers.'

How fortunate that his successors understood his original vision so well, and Waddesdon is now a model for a National Trust house where the family are prepared to more than subsidise it and have aesthetic influence. Today, the house is in immaculate order after a long period of repair and maintenance that began in 1984. For several years, as the roof was renewed along with all the plumbing, wiring and security, the house had to be closed to the public. Major changes took place on the first floor including the installation of discovered but unused *boiseries* from Parisian hôtels, in newly created rooms designed with the assistance of architect Peter Inskip and interior designer David Mlinaric. The

The White Drawing Room now
displaying the silver service made
for George III

The Blue Dining Room, now containing Ingo Maurer's contemporary chandelier *Porca Miseria*, commissioned in 2003

The Smoking Room in the Bachelors' Wing at the Manor, restored to its 19th-century splendour during the Centenary restoration

Opposite: Rothschild vernacular architecture in Waddesdon village – the school and Institute

Smoking Room, Blue Sitting Room, the Red Ante-Room, the White Drawing Room and the Blue Dining Room were just some of the recreated rooms. Everything that was done to the house was a successful continuation of the clear policy for the house and estate with a return to the high pre-war standards of care and display.

This approach also applied to the grounds and gardens on a grand scale. A two-thousand-yard long avenue of oak trees was planted to mark the Millennium; the main parterre was replanted; the Aviary was restored and contemporary sculpture acquired. Woods and hedgerows have been renewed and the gardens and walks all upgraded.

The estate buildings by W F Taylor, including the stables at Eythrope and the Five Arrows in the village, all developed an 'Old English Domestic style' adding to the rich idiosyncratic approach to rural architecture at Waddesdon.

In the review of buildings it has always seemed right to conserve the buildings of

The ornamental Dairy on the estate, designed by W F Taylor

architectural importance and take the opportunity to create some new ones.

In 1994, it was decided to adapt the Dairy building on the estate so that it could be used to generate income from conferences and weddings, and a superb conversion was carried out by Isabel and Julian Bannerman. Their especial expertise is garden design and they saw the potential with Lord Rothschild for the lakeside gardens restored and boathouses created as a waterside setting for entertaining. The Dairy has retained a feeling of elegant rusticity in a beautifully planted setting.

On the estate several farms and their associated buildings recently came under review. Three particular sites – Model Farm, Beachendon Farm and Windmill Hill Farm – were in need of renewal and more productive uses, following the decision to dispose of the estate's dairy enterprises, and provided an opportunity to commission some creative new architecture. At Windmill Hill, the farm buildings had until very recently been used for dairy farming which was in serious commercial decline. It was suggested that architects should look at the potential of all three sites, and also a low-lying derelict farm site at Common Leys, to consider ways of regeneration. All this activity was directed at finding the best ways to continue the pursuit of perfection for the whole estate in ways to ensure its future viability. The 500 acres of grass historically occupied by the dairy herd has now been amalgamated into the existing arable crop rotation and the existing beef and sheep herds. The demolition of the industrial style portal frame farm buildings will considerably enhance the visual qualities of the estate.

A contemporary version of a family mausoleum in the Manor gardens, *Terra degli Etruschi* made in 2000 by Stephen Cox

WINDMILL HILL

THE ARCHITECTURAL STORY

Finding the right architect is always key to the success of a project and the selection process, while subject to personal taste, has to be seen to be fair and open. The search for the right architect for the three sites that needed renewal on the estate had produced some interesting very early submissions. It was finally decided in late 2007 to initiate the renewal process on one site up on the breezy heights of Windmill Hill where the dairy herd was gradually being disbanded and the group of barns and farm buildings were not of any major architectural significance. The emerging brief for the site was clear in its wish to create a facility which would provide a centralised archive store for records relating to Waddesdon Manor, its collections, the papers of Yad Hanadiv outside Israel, and of the four generations of the Rothschild family who have worked to ensure that Waddesdon is preserved, protected and developed for the benefit of the public. This facility was from the beginning intended to be widely accessible for study and as an ongoing support to the Manor.

Like all architectural briefs it evolved through lengthy debate and discussion. Initially consideration was given to the provision of some residential accommodation for visiting scholars and a house for the director of the collections. These thoughts may have generated the idea of building in a collegiate way around courtyards, but eventually it was decided to house the offices of The Rothschild Foundation on the site and possibly to build a director's house elsewhere. Key elements of the final brief that would be submitted for planning consent always included substantial archive storage with appropriate environmental controls; a reading room large enough for meetings and small conferences; office and seminar space with room for future growth of the archives.

The buildings on Windmill Hill are part of the innovative approach to the development of the estate to prepare it for the rapidly changing world of the twenty-first century. In the search for the architect it was key to find one who understood the need to build for a dynamic future while respecting the particular qualities that make Waddesdon outstanding.

The choice of Stephen Marshall Architects from a long short list of candidates was

Overall plan of the Estate

Former hayloft from previous agricultural use at Windmill Hill farm. The layering of the materials forming the elevation and the corrugated tin roof influenced the elevations of the new Archive centre.

Timber-framed, wood-clad barn used for storing hay and cattle feed. The structural form of this space influenced the roof structure of the new Reading Room.

particularly inspired by the work he had done for the New Art Centre at Roche Court in Wiltshire, as well as by the high standard of his design approach. Roche Court is a fine Regency house built in 1804, and is set in a sloping park surrounded by woods which are now successfully used as a sculpture park and garden. The New Art Centre run by Madeleine, Lady Bessborough, moved to Wiltshire from London and now has space for major outdoor exhibitions and educational programmes. Stephen Marshall was initially asked to join the existing Orangery to the house by building an elegant roofed gallery along an existing wall. The lightweight roof appears to float and allows light to flood in along the old wall making perfect conditions for the display of art. Subsequent works at Roche Court include an Artist's House – inspired by Kettle's Yard in Cambridge – a new Cube gallery for the display of small sculpture, and improvements to the catering area and kitchen. The Artist's House, set in a courtyard, allows for showing works of art in a domestic setting. All these new additions to an old house on a fine estate are sensitive and completely contemporary, and utilise a limited but appropriate palette of materials, stone, concrete, glass and oak. In scale, they relate perfectly to both the park and the Regency house. The Gallery has won many awards, including the RIBA, *Stephen Lawrence Award*; the Royal Fine Art Commission *Building of the Year Commendation* and many others.

Stephen Marshall was born in 1956 and trained as an architect at Glasgow's Strathclyde University (B.Arch. 1979). He was a Harkness Fellow at Harvard University Graduate School of Design in 1982, where his MA thesis was on the role of parks and gardens in urban design. He has worked with Terry Farrell and partners and in partnership for some years with Alfred Munkenbeck. Today his practice, Stephen Marshall Architects LLP, London, carries out a range of architectural work including private houses, high-density urban housing – some for students – and buildings for the arts and some competition entries. Historically, when in partnership with Munkenbeck, the firm worked on the Visitor's Centre at Mount Stuart on the Isle of Bute and the Jerwood Sculpture gallery in the converted stables at Ragley Hall in Warwickshire.

Is there a defined language that is recognisably the handwriting of Stephen Marshall? While it naturally varies according to the site, he has evolved an enriched simplicity of design where an almost abstract formality is enhanced by rich natural materials. His particular skill is to clarify the key advantages of a site and, in the making of a new place, define it in an original way – for example by creating a sense of enclosure, the use of water, reflection and bold landscaping. He also achieves structural simplicity and very logical planning. At Roche Court, on a much smaller scale, he has also demonstrated that it is possible and indeed desirable to add buildings of the finest contemporary quality to existing historic buildings. Marshall's work is harmonious in its simplicity.

Exterior view of the sculpture gallery at Roche Court connecting the original house with the listed orangery

Interior view of the sculpture gallery at the New Art Centre, Roche Court

The Artist's House at Roche Court. Simple render walls with oak opening shutters. The low level external shelf is for small-scale outdoor sculpture.

Opposite: Cube Gallery at Roche Court

Glass cube window to bathroom above shallow reflecting pool

Interior view of the stable conversion
at Westwell Manor

The entrance to Dulwich Pond and Park House

Southern terrace at Dulwich Pond and Park
House. Formed in extended format grey
brick, oak, aluminium and limestone.

Bird's-eye view of the Manor House with Windmill Hill to the right of the image

THE EVOLUTION OF THE DESIGN

From the beginning the site, with its extensive views at Windmill Hill, has dictated the form and plan of the new buildings. The footprint of the extensive barns indicated the sort of area that could be available for new buildings. The decision to keep a small part of the best-looking tiled barns was to have a visual effect on the proposals for new tiled roofs on part of the site. The views of the site from other parts of the estate suggested that the roofline should be relatively low and this was also predicated by the height of the retained barn.

To achieve the atmosphere of calm reflection the plan from the very start had two courtyards divided by the large double-height reading room at the very centre of the scheme. The large entrance courtyard has a formality in its garden (now planted with *Amelanchier Taxus*) and almost the key element of the entire scheme is the great opening to the sweeping view of the landscape to the west. The second courtyard with its rolling lawn has a more austere atmosphere, surrounded as it is by archives, but also a superb view to the south.

The double courtyard scheme won enthusiastic planning consent from Aylesbury Vale District Council in July 2008. In August of that year a report was written on the landscape and the approach by road to the site which successfully advocated a new route:

> '*in the spirit of the kind of "Improvements" envisaged by landscape artists like Capability Brown and Humphry Repton it would seem to be a good idea to consider moving the final stretch of the approach road to the north-western higher ground – adopting this higher new road approach will give the visitor the opportunity to enjoy exceptional views, that, until now, have not been very accessible.*'

This recommendation was adopted and, combined with the decision to remove all overhead cables and place services underground, made it clear that the aesthetics of the countryside were always going to be paramount at Waddesdon.

Equally important to the success of the Windmill Hill scheme has been a sustainable approach. Ground source heat pumps and grey water recycling contribute to this, and the Archives themselves have been constructed on a passive control principle using massively thick insulating walls.

As the scheme has evolved on the site architecturally, the opportunity has been taken to enhance the buildings with works from the collection of contemporary art and sculpture. Specially designed furniture has been purchased for the Reading Room and a lighting scheme devised to enhance the remarkable oak ceiling. Archival storage will meet the highest environmental standards and office and seminar facilities will be of the highest standard. The Rothschild Foundation is the main occupant of the north building where flexible office space has been designed.

Marshall Architects have worked with Mary Keen and Pip Morrison on the landscaping of the scheme with some advice as well from The Landscape Agency. As the trees grow, the setting will be sylvan, and visitors to the building will have driven along the new scenic route crossing the Millennium avenue into the reflective green courts of the new home of the benevolent charitable activities of The Rothschild Foundation, and the historical records of a remarkable house, family and collection.

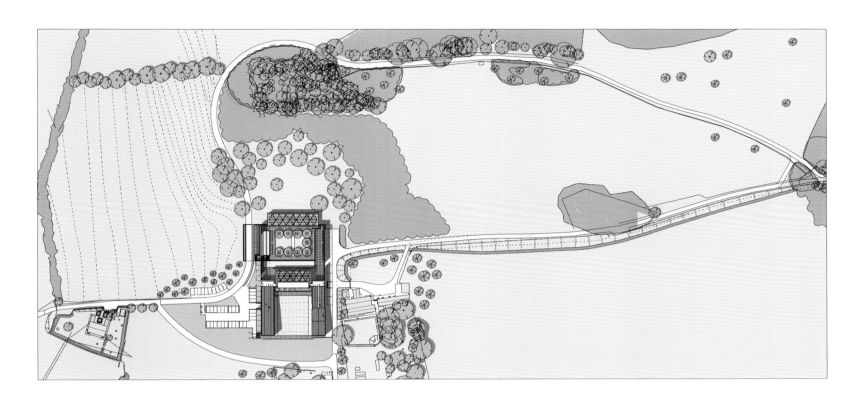

Site plan with new access road to the north

The new Archive complex from the air

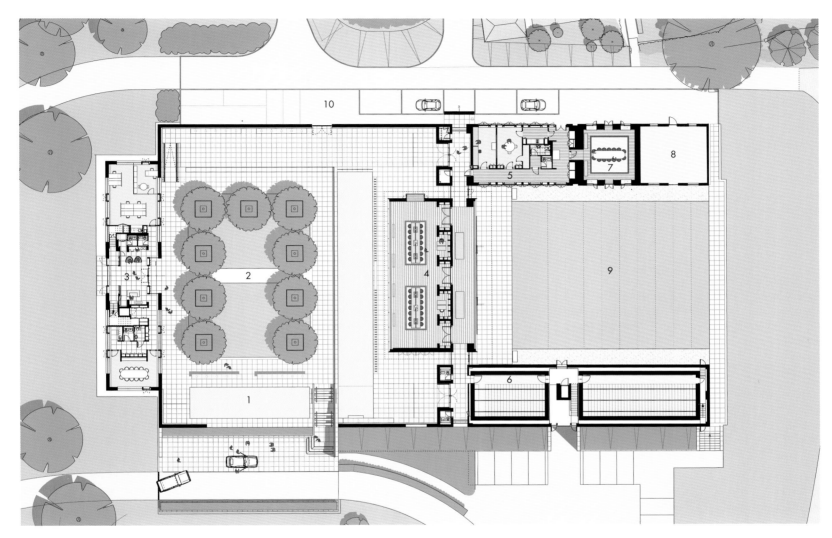

Ground Floor Plan

1. Entry courtyard
2. Central courtyard
3. Office building
4. Reading Room
5. Archive Office
6. Archive Storage
7. Project Room
8. Plant Room
9. Rolling lawn
10. Eastern Gate

The Archive building set beside the existing Windmill Hill farmhouse

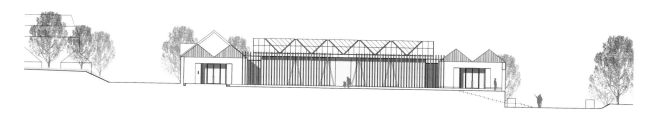

Elevation AA. Showing zinc roofs, oak screen to the reading room and entrance / terrace wings

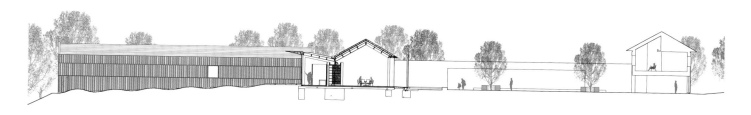

Section BB. Showing section through central courtyard reading room and rolling lawn. Archive storage building in background

Elevation CC. Flying Beam to entrance courtyard and oak-clad archive storage building on right

The central courtyard is approached by steps leading from the arrival courtyard. The steps are positioned between the two reflective pools. The oak screen to the Reading Room can be seen through the framed view.

The view west out to Ashendon is framed by the flying beam. Views of the sky
and clouds open out. The reflective pools double as fire brigade tanks.

View of the office building with angled zinc roof-screen. Openings in the office elevation are formed from oak cladding, oak shutters and glass. The free-standing oak screen provides shade and privacy to the reading room, its form based on the cowshed screens previously on the Windmill farm site.

Looking across the central courtyard to the Reading Room, the oak screen is divided to give direct views through to the south. The landscaping is formal in direct contrast to the more open wild countryside of Windmill Hill.

The main entrance to the Archive building. The pitched roofs are based on those on the adjacent farmhouse.
The bronze sculpture, *A couple of differences between thinking and feeling*, is by Angus Fairhurst.

Looking west through the service gates formed in oak. The stone to the courtyard is basalt and was imported from northern China.

Overleaf: The architecture of the courtyard buildings reflects the former agricultural use at Windmill Hill. Roofs are finished in zinc, walls are rendered and louvres and shutters are formed in oak. The Reading Room screen is free-standing and cantilevers from the ground.

Opposite: The screen from angle, closed view.

Above: The screen straight on, open view.

Overleaf: Looking over the arrival courtyard through the flying beam to the central courtyard beyond.

Looking across the courtyard to the office building. The small oak doors at low level of Reading Room provide natural cross-ventilation reducing energy use.

Entrance opposite Windmill Hill Farmhouse leads to the Reading Room.

View from south to viewing point on western Reading Room terrace

The steps up to the courtyard with
Reading Room beyond

The reception to Reading Room with
antique marble column in background

Entrance to Archive/Reading Room
with solid ledged and braced
shutters. The Fairhurst bronze
sculpture is reflected.

South gallery space with timber gridshell roof. The gridshell is supported on columns set within the large oak doors opening onto the terrace. *Mad Dogs* by Alison Read, 1994, comprises five papier-mâché sculptures.

Opposite: A–section through Reading Room and south gallery space showing gridshell structure. Apart from small locating brackets the roof structure is entirely wood, similar in construction to the timber-framed barn previously on the site.

Overleaf: The Reading Room with wall lights 'Broken Dreams', by Fernando and Humberto Campana. The tables within the space were designed by the architects and can be removed allowing room for conference seating. *A couple of differences between thinking and feeling* looks on.

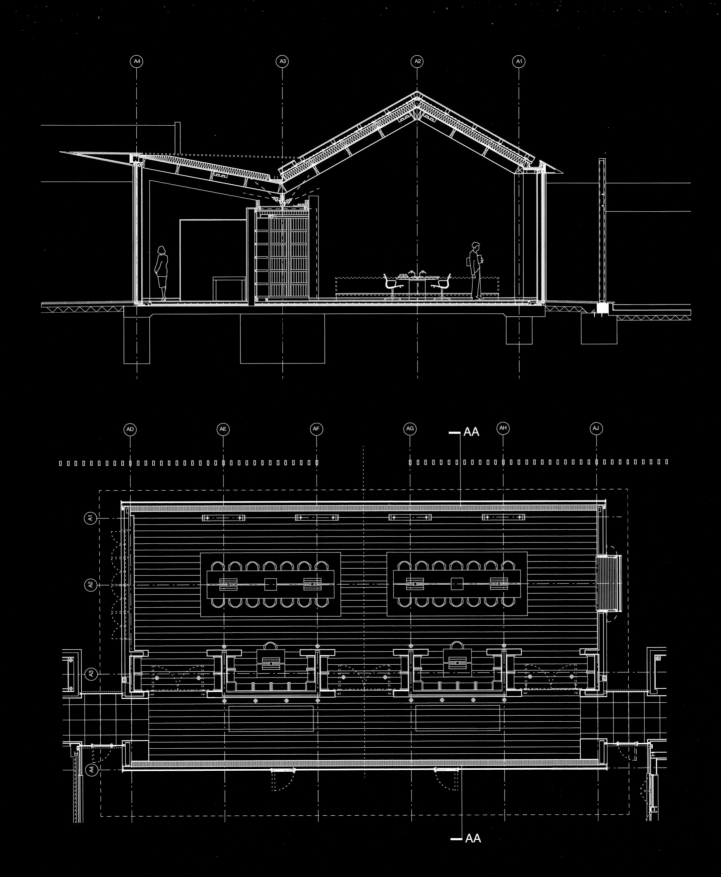

The view looking south framed by the Campana brothers' lights. All lighting in the Reading Room is hidden and is designed to wash the oak surfaces giving a soft edge to the space.

View to central courtyard from
the Reading Room

At night, the central space is designed as an outdoor room and the lighting is designed to give the feeling of an internal space.

Looking across the courtyard to the office building from the Reading Room

Detail of custom-designed light units, recessed into oak gridshell. Each light is designed for the different modes of use within the space – reading, meetings, conferences and lectures.

Recessed light emphasises the triangular geometry of the roof structure.

The timber diagrid is one of the largest in the UK. The structure of the pitched roofs acts like angled trusses, which give very long spans with minimal material.

The roof being assembled under a temporary roof on site

Opposite top. Reading Room roof plan.
Opposite bottom: Reflected ceiling plan of gridshell showing reading room, southern Gallery and zinc 'nose-cone' trim to the roof.

Overleaf: The Reading Room at night. The space is lit like a large outdoor room.

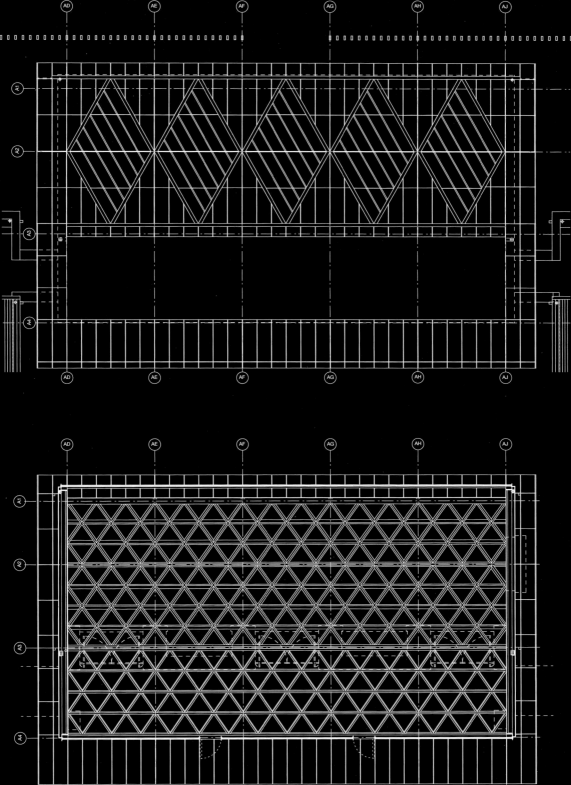

Interior of the archive stores. They have a functional, passively controlled environment using minimum energy, an important factor in archive storage.

Opposite: The existing stable building was retained within the archive group and is now used as a special project room. The wall panel is by Edward Bawden, 'English Garden Delights', *circa* 1947. The panel was originally made for the salon of the liner *Orcades*.

Looking over the rolling lawn towards the Reading Room. The archive storage building is on the left with the retained farm buildings on the right. The projecting zinc 'nose-cone' gives shade to the southern gallery space.

The rolling lawn is designed as a very large 'recliner'. In good weather it will be possible to sit out and enjoy the southerly view. The double-height door with integral structure can be seen in the background.

The Archive office building is designed to fit in with the retained farm buildings and the farmhouse beyond.

Opposite: Oak door access to the southern terrace

Exterior of office building seen from the Archive Reading Room

The Reading Room from the office building entrance

Office Reception

Conference Room with
oak shutters

Looking down to central courtyard from office building balcony, the farmhouse roofs are on the left in the distance.

Baron Ferdinand's
Red Book, a record
of the house and
its contents in
1897

A HOME FOR WADDESDON'S ARCHIVES

The creation of the Archive and Reading Room at Windmill Hill allows Waddesdon's immensely rich documentary resources to be drawn together for the first time in a way which makes them more accessible to researchers and the public. Waddesdon's history unfolds through its archives, and the collections relate in particular to the members of the Rothschild family who created and have cared for Waddesdon, from Baron Ferdinand de Rothschild who built the Manor to the present Lord Rothschild, who manages it today on behalf of the National Trust. They also reflect the many and varied interests of the family as these have developed over time.

The Rothschilds are famous for their activities as collectors and connoisseurs, but this is only one aspect of their history which can be traced through the archival collections. Just as interesting for scholars of 19th-century social and agricultural history is the material relating to the running of the Estate, during a period convulsed by two world wars after which the social fabric of Britain was changed forever. When Baron Ferdinand bought the Waddesdon estate in 1874, and began to build the Manor, his intention was to create a place to which he could retreat from London and entertain family and friends at his famous weekend house parties. Everything at Waddesdon, from the spectacular collection and immaculately kept gardens, to the malmaison carnations in the glass houses, the butter in the Dairy and the prize-winning cattle, was of the highest possible standard. This commitment to excellence was continued by Miss Alice de Rothschild, Ferdinand's sister, who inherited the Manor in 1889, whose passion for horticulture is revealed in a fascinating series of letters to her Head

Baron Edmond, with his son and daughter-in-law James and Dorothy de Rothschild, on a visit to
Israel around 1920

Gardener, George Johnson. It was Alice who steered Waddesdon through the First World
War and who witnessed the beginnings of a change in emphasis and management. She
was followed by her French great-nephew, James de Rothschild and his young English wife
Dorothy, whose passions, racing and golf, were reflected in the creation of a stud and a golf
course. In the years after the Second World War, it was James who began the negotiations
with the National Trust which were to culminate in the bequest, in 1957, of the Manor, its
principal contents, and its gardens.

Thereafter, Waddesdon was open to the public, under the direction of James's widow
Dorothy, and this period of administration and governance by the National Trust and the

Alice de Rothschild, Ferdinand's sister and heir

A rare early autochrome of Alice's sitting room at the Manor, taken around 1910

Rothschild charitable trusts which were set up to manage the Manor on the National Trust's behalf, is another rich documentary resource. A number of philanthropic Trusts have now been brought together to form a single charity, The Rothschild Foundation, whose grant-giving activities now also have a home at Windmill Hill.

There is also another important strand of Rothschild family history which can be explored through the Waddesdon Archives, as a result of James's inheritance of the Manor. He was the eldest son of Baron Edmond de Rothschild, Ferdinand and Alice's cousin,

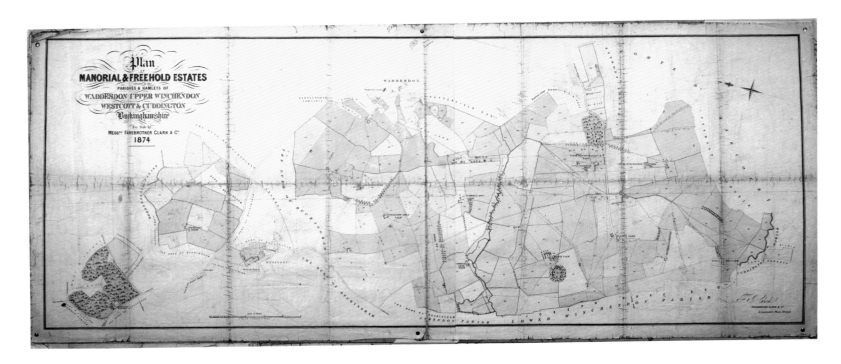

A plan of the Waddesdon estate as acquired by Baron Ferdinand in 1874 showing Lodge Hill, the future site of the Manor

whose collections and papers on his death were divided between his three children. James's inheritance included the administrative records of PICA (the Palestine Jewish Colonisation Association), set up by Baron Edmond in 1882 as a response to the plight of Jews displaced from Russia, providing resources to buy land and build homes and to encourage agricultural self-sufficiency. The Baron had an enduring commitment to Palestine, an interest shared and developed by James, who took on the presidency of PICA until his death. Its successor organisation, Yad Hanadiv, an educational and philanthropic foundation which continues to this day, was initially chaired by Dorothy and, under her auspices, several major projects were undertaken, one of the most significant being the building of the Supreme Court of Israel.

The Head Groom and his staff photographed in the Stables Courtyard around 1900

Once re-housed, these varied collections will be catalogued and gradually be made available on-line. The archives already underpin understanding of Waddesdon and the ways in which its many facets are brought alive for its visitors, but the potential offered by a new, purpose-built building will allow scholars and the public world-wide to enjoy its rich resources. From art and horticulture to social and agricultural history, from wine to estate management, from the history and politics of Israel to the protocol of a visit by Queen Victoria, all this and more can be explored through the creation at Windmill Hill.

Overleaf: The central courtyard looking west at sunset

CREDITS AND ACKNOWLEDGMENTS

This book was made to celebrate the creation of the new Archives, Reading Room and home of The Rothschild Foundation at Windmill Hill on the Waddesdon Estate, and to accompany an exhibition about the new building at the Coach House at the Manor in 2011. First and foremost, thanks are due to Lord Rothschild, without whose creative energy Windmill Hill would not exist. Also to Fabia Bromovsky, whose guidance as Chief Executive at Waddesdon brought the project to fruition, and Edward Parsons, the Project Manager. Many others have helped to make the vision become reality, and this book is a tribute to them all.

In particular, thanks are due to:
For the building: Stephen Marshall Architects LLP, including Stephen Marshall, Sam Coley, Yiannis Kanakakis, Colin Amery (Architectural Consultant). Structural Surveyors – Thornton Tomasetti including Les Postawa, Michael Roberts. Environmental Consultants – Max Fordham including Henry Luker, Neil Smith, Ruggiero Guida, Kai Salman–Lord. Lighting design – Speirs and Major Associates including Mark Major, Chris Beasley. Quantity Surveyor – Selway Joyce, including Ian McCoy, Nick Tarrier, Hui Meng, Ed Smith. Landscape Designers – Mary Keen and Philip Morrison. The Landscape Agency – Alistair Baldwin, Matthew Jarvis and Stuart Postlethwaite. Landscaping – Elmtree Construction – Bruce Clark and Dick Hopkins.
Interior Design: David Mlinaric
For construction: Main Contractor, Kingerlee Ltd, including Paul Hardy, Tom Howdill, Rob Cruickshank, Jim Jewers, Steve Worley, Mark Watterson. Joinery – A. Edmonds & Co. Ltd including David Edmonds, The Green Oak Carpentry Company Ltd, including Steve Corbett. Zinc roof – PJB Cladding Services Ltd including Oliver Bromley. Electrical subcontractor – RT Harris & Son Ltd, including Stuart Davies. Commercial Stone. Mechanical subcontractor – F.G. Alden Ltd including Dave Hale. Glazing subcontractor – Solaglas Ltd including Richard Wiletts. Archive internal joinery – Hannaford/ Kingerlee Joinery. Archive fit out – Rackline, including Aidan Moss. CCTV – Chiltern Technology, including Graham Johnson. Access Control and Alarms – i2 Security, including Adrian Beesley and Matt Long. Fire safety – Tecserve, including Faye Ridley, Martyn White, Mark Painter. Telecommunications – Bluebell Telecoms Ltd, including Derek Brown, Chris Hollins, Billy Greward. Environmental consultants – Bernwood ECS Ltd, including Chris Damant. Environmental control – Triple Pole, including Andy Morrison, Volvina, including Mark Stewart. Furniture: Donal Channer & Co

Photography: Richard Bryant / arcaidimages.com

From Waddesdon Manor: Fabia Bromovsky, Edward Parsons and the Estate Team, Les Duff, Paul Farnell, Richard Ernst, Andy Batten and the Gardens Department, Julie Chadwell, Dave Silvester, Mark Hyland, Naomi Hicks, Colette Warbrick, Jane Finch, Katie Vials, Matthew Waters, Harriet Nichols, Hazel Friend, Paul Worsley, John Thurlow, Brian Wheeler and the Maintenance Department, Vicky Darby, Kim Hallett, Diane Bellis, Jill Geber, Nicola Allen, Sophieke Piebenga, Ashley Jones, Alastair Brooks, June Primmer, Fiona Sinclair, Milly Soames (and Super Ted!)

For the exhibition: Rachel Boak, Emily Roy, Yiannis Kanakakis, Jane Cliffe, Dirty Design, Jane Rick (Spencer House), Chris Beasley (Speirs and Major), Central Electrics, Ian Thomson (Thomsons), Paul Knibb, Spittles
The authors would particularly like to thank the following for their help with this book:
Michael Mitchell and Susan Wightman of Libanus Press, Rachel Boak, Emily Roy, Jane Rick, Richard Bryant, Yiannis Kanakakis, Melanie Aspey (The Rothschild Archive) and Sally Berkowitz (The Rothschild Foundation, Europe).

BIBLIOGRAPHY

Amery, Colin, *A Celebration of Art and Architecture – National Gallery Sainsbury Wing* National Gallery Publications, distributed by Yale University Press (1991)

Crookham, Alan, *The National Gallery: An illustrated history* National Gallery Company Ltd., distributed by Yale University Press (2009)

Friedman, Joseph, *Spencer House: Chronicle of a Great London Mansion* with a Foreword by Lord Rothschild, Zwemmer, (1993)

Gurney, Ivor and Carr, Norman, *Waddesdon Through the Ages,* The Alice Trust (2004)

Hall, Michael, *Waddesdon Manor: The Heritage of a Rothschild House* Scala Publishers Ltd, (2009)

National Trust *Waddesdon Manor – Guide* (1994)

The Waddesdon Companion Guide text by Selma Schwartz – 3rd revised edition contributions by Rachel Boak and Pippa Shirley (2008)

Pons, Bruno, *The James A. de Rothschild Collection at Waddesdon Manor: Architecture and Panelling* Philip Wilson Publishers Ltd, (1996)

de Rothschild, Mrs James *The Rothschilds at Waddesdon Manor* William Collins & Co Ltd, (1979)

Sharon, Yosef *The Supreme Court Building , Jerusalem* Yad Hanadiv (1993)

JOURNALS

Apollo, July/August 2007, Interview with Lord Rothschild by Michael Hall.

Country Life, February 16 & 23 1989, The Rothschilds in the Vale of Aylesbury Parts I and II by Jill Allibone.

PHOTOGRAPHIC CREDITS

P.6 © Lucian Freud Photo: Mike Fear

Pp.9–10 © The Rothschild Foundation Photos: Mike Fear

P.11 © The Hyatt Foundation

P.12 © City of London

P.15 © Spencer House Limited Photo: Mark Fiennes

P.16 © Spencer House Limited Photo: Mark Fiennes

P.17 © Christie's Images 2010

P.26 © Paul Benney Photo: Mike Fear

P.27 ©Ada Karmi-Melamede and Ram Karmi

P.30 © The National Trust, Waddesdon Manor
    Photo: John Bigelow Taylor

P.32 © The National Trust, Waddesdon Manor
    Photo: John Thomson; © Ben Swartz

P.34 © The National Trust, Waddesdon Manor
    Photo: Mike Fear

P.35 © The National Trust, Waddesdon Manor
    Photo: John Bigelow Taylor

P.36 © The National Trust, Waddesdon Manor
    Photo: John Bigelow Taylor

P.37 © The National Trust, Waddesdon Manor

P.38 © The National Trust, Waddesdon Manor
    Photo: John Bigelow Taylor

P.39 © Stephen Cox Photo: John Bigelow Taylor

P.40 © The National Trust, Waddesdon Manor
    Photo: John Bigelow Taylor

P.43 and P.45 Stephen Marshall Architects

P.46 and p.48 Arcaid

P.52 © 2011 Google Maps

P.88 Stephen Marshall Architects

P.102 © The National Trust, Waddesdon Manor
    Photo: John Bigelow Taylor

P.103 © The National Trust, Waddesdon Manor

P.105 – Both: © The National Trust, Waddesdon Manor

P.106 © The National Trust, Waddesdon Manor
    Photo: Mike Fear

P.107 © The National Trust, Waddesdon Manor